The Forest of Darkness

Alan Hodgkinson

Published by Eastern Eagle Books, 2024.

THE FOREST OF DARKNESS

First edition. February 19, 2024.

ISBN: 979-8224117314

Written by Alan Hodgkinson.

Table of Contents

PREFACE

As the plane lifted off the tarmac of Fairfield Air Force Base, I mentally crossed my fingers. Our Pan American plane, I later learned, was chartered by an outfit called Air America. I looked out the window watching Fairfield become a shrinking grid work of roads, houses and surrounding farmlands. Soon we were over the Bay Area. Far below, Bay Area. Far below, at Eastbay, you could just make out the bell tower of U.C. Berkeley. I had been one of the hippies protesting the war there, only six months past the Summer of Love. What were us Americans doing there in

Southeast Asia, killing the little yellow men? Us thousands of protestors ended up one night bottlenecked on leather sandaled footwear at Sather Gate, trying to gain entrance to the campus. We planned to take over the university. The hundreds of police with their tear gas, not hip on our riotous behavior, kept us at bay. Presently, what was I doing going to go fight in that war I so much opposed? So young and naïve, and with so much to learn about life, I had to smile to myself at this psychological whiplash from then to now, that awakened me with a much greater force than the four jet engines launching me skyward. I was just a nineteen-year-old kid. What the hell did I really know about the subject of war and peace?

CHAPTER I: PARADISE BULLET RIDDLED

Within several days, I found myself at a place called Long Binh, just north of Saigon. This would be my jumping off point for my assignment to a unit somewhere in Vietnam. The replacement center provided service much like a stateside employment office, matching your documented skills and education with a job. Outside of that, you would have little choice, and if you didn't like your assignment by some damned desk jokey, you could throw a child-like fit, and insist on getting a more favorable placement, likely to no avail. The U.S. Army was never a user-friendly, equal opportunity employer, and anyone who thought different was misinformed. You got your orders, and simply fit into them. However, there is an inkling of choice before you got your orders.

A trip by bus with wire-mesh protected windows transported us. I watched out my window along the way, marveling at the beautiful tropical scenery, mainly of coconut trees. In a short time it turned into a dense rubber tree plantation with their own scenic luster at our drop-off point. A guy in regular jungle fatigues directed me and the others from the bus, still in our colorful civies fresh from California, to a barracks. He pointed to us the mess hall building telling us meal hours, second most important pointing out a bunker for the surrounding barracks, and finally told us several dozen newbies we would be processed the next day.

Inside the two-story building, I found a bunk for myself and settled in for my first night in Vietnam. I quickly conked out from the long trip, but in a short time became abruptly awakened by the loud booming of outgoing artillery, or perhaps fairly close incoming mortars-as a newbie, I could not say for sure.

The guys in the other bunks, perhaps more knowing, scrambled.

I was certain to get to the nearest bunker in case it was incoming. I was too tired to move. My thought, in comic relief to myself was: I wonder how a guy can even get any sleep around this place?

I spent several days at the replacement center, policing cigarette butts from the barracks grounds as per instruction of low ranking, loudmouthed kids with no MOS yet, and running errands for anyone who outranked me—as in everyone. A Specialist-four in starched fatigues and spit-shined boots, approached me while I was sweeping the barracks floor, as instructed by one of the before mentioned minions in olive-greens. This kid, about my age and appearance of blond hair and blue eyes could have been my brother asked me, "Do you know where private Hodgkinson is?"

I stopped sweeping and stared back at him, "Who wants to know?"

"The main man in charge. The master sergeant."

"I'm Hodgkinson," I admitted.

"Well, put that broom down. I'm here to instruct you to report to the master sergeant's office-pronto. I'll show you where it is."

This would be no doubt be the moment of truth regarding my job placement in Vietnam. As I walked the short distance to the admin building behind the guy, I felt a sting on the back of my neck. I slapped that place hard. Looking at the palm of my hand, I beheld a splotch of blood. Mosquitoes, I swore. Little fucking vampires! Between the mortar attacks, the Vietnamese mosquitoes and everyone telling me what to do, I had no doubt this place was going to be a real kick in the ass.

Known by any of my acquaintances back home for a person deciding his own destiny in face of all odds, I thought to myself, "Don't let the Army deal you a bad hand." Inside the admin building, behind the desk of the master sergeant, sitting in a wooden chair front and center, I watched as he went through the several pages that constituted my military file. He looked up at me after a minute.

"Your five months of training at Ft. Lewis, the icing on top three months of advanced infantry schooling says all over the place, to hand this guy an M-16 to go out and kill gooks. I'll be assigning you to an infantry unit to that purpose. It'll take several days to get you processed. Any questions?"

"Yeah. Can I be in Long Range Reconnaissance Patrol?"

This man, administratively in charge of what came down to my life and death in service to my country, stared at me long.

"You understand what you're asking, volunteering for the LRRPs? We'll have to send you to an academy. The LRRPs are an elite bunch. They don't want no Beetle Bailys. In the academy, you're pretty much going for a master's degree in Eleven-charlie. What makes you think you're equal to the task?"

I shrugged. "You've got my paperwork. It should tell you of my merit. I fired sharpshooter in basic, completed AIT, was invited to become a helicopter pilot because of my IQ. I'm no lightweight."

"You make a good case for yourself. I'll put in the paperwork and you'll hear from me soon. Meanwhile, get back to what you were doing."

Nothing that will earn me an Army Commendation Metal, I felt like saying, in reference to my chore of sweeping floors.

One among us in holding pattern, still in civies approached me while I was policing cigarette butts. "Hey dude, are you getting bummed out with the garrison BS?"

I had met him on the bus ride, and learned he was a fellow Californian.

"Appreciate you noticed my situation."

"Well, I was just talking to a truck driver. He's getting supplies from Ton Se Nhut in a little while and offered me a ride to downtown Saigon. He said he's got room for one more than me. Like I'm saying, would you like to go to Saigon for a couple of hours of cold beer and female company?"

"Show me the way," I replied.

In a short time, we arrived downtown Saigon just thirty miles south. The truck driver stopped at the curb and pointed out his favorite nightclub. "The girls here are out-of-sight, and most all of them speak English."

His advice was good, and we had a fun time with girls hanging all over us at the bar and rock music playing loud. After three San Miguels with a beautiful teenage girl lap dancing me, I decided that Vietnam wasn't such a bad place, of course unless an unpinned hand grenade rolled into the bar -as it occurred occasionally in Saigon. After several hours, the truck driver easily found us, and it was back to the real world of Long Bihn. Reclining on my bunk, the spec-four errand boy of the day before approached. His hands were on his hips. "Your presence is desired at the master sergeant's office. Right now."

I rolled out of the bunk bed and promptly made the several minute long trip, expecting to hear the fate of my prospects of becoming a LLRP. The master sergeant didn't ask me to sit down. He looked angry. "I got an approval for your application to LLRP school. I had my errand boy trying to find you all day. Where've been?"

"Oh, I took a break from my menial chores and had a few beers down in Saigon. I was only gone three or so hours," I said defensively.

"Without my permission! That break that you took, by any other words is what we call AWOL. He had some paperwork in hand and tore it in half, letting it down to his desktop. "That was your LLRP orders. I should haul your ass to LBJ for a month stay. You know what LBJ is?"

I had heard in my short time at the replacement center. "Long Bihn Jail."

"That's right. But that would be too nice. What I'm going to do is assign you too the worse outfit in the Army by count of body bags. That battalion in the Mekong Delta has been begging me for more men because of their gut-wrenching attrition. They're called the 3/60th, Ninth Infantry Division. You go AWOL from them, the commanding officer will have you shot just to set an example and blame your death on the VC.

"Wow. Thanks for the special attention."

He handed me my orders. "Pack your things. You'll be leaving by deuce and a half at dawn. Now get the hell out of my face."

The following morning the two-and-a-half-ton truck hauled me along with a load of other Fucking New Guys (*FNGs,* I was learning some army vernacular), destination Dong Tam base camp in the Mekong Delta.

Around three hours of bumpy dirt road, us teenage privates and slightly older pair of lieutenants arrived at the headquarters building of Ninth Infantry Division. I went inside the plank building and showed my orders to a sergeant behind an impressively sanded and oiled hardwood counter. He took several minutes to get me a weapon and handed it over like you were getting potato chips and a can of beer at a convenience store.

"You'll get your ammo and grenades, etcetera when you join up with your new unit."

I shouldered the obviously used M-16 by its polyester strap. "Just wondering, what's with that pile of fatigues and gear out front?"

"Two companies were hit pretty hard in the past week. Each pair of boots denotes a KIA, or WIA. A detail is just now going through the clothes for personal effects to send home using dog tags for return address and pilfer out field gear we can reuse before we burn all else. Those piles are beginning to appear too often from being dropped off from medivac copters at the field hospital nearby. What outfit are you assigned to?"

"Uh, Alpha Company."

The supply sergeant stared at me in a moment of silence.

"That's who you are, among other FNGs, are replacing. That pile represents a bunch of boys from Alpha and Bravo Company. Count the boots in that pile and divide by two. That's the number of them you'll come up with. Welcome to the Ninth Division.

Ever since the Vietnam bound plane lifted off from Fairfield two weeks past, I had been in holding pattern for a roundhouse punch that would mentally knock me off my feet. All this gave credence to my angst. After likely dozens of such landings to that Southeast Asian war theater at his control-stick, aware that he had another plane weighed in every seat with passengers on edge at the possible consequences of what they would be facing at their destination, the pilot no doubt felt it appropriate to lighten the mood. As the airliner speeded down the tarmac in takeoff, the pilot came over the PA. "Welcome aboard our flight from Fairfield, California to Saigon, Vietnam. If your planned destination is not Saigon, I can't help you at this point, but I can drop you off at one of our refueling stopovers at Hawaii, Midway Island or Manila. Meanwhile, sit back and enjoy your flight. The stewardess will be coming around with drinks."

A nineteen-year-old draftee, I had spent months of training at Fort Lewis, and tried to stay calm about my inevitable tour of a warzone. I wouldn't know my military occupation until I arrived in Vietnam. I had prayed that I would be assigned a desk job in Saigon, the bastion of bountiful juicy, young Asian girls. Wishful thinking. Worst case scenario, the army would throw this milky kid to the wolves to a combat unit. You might end up getting captured and be repeatedly tortured and held in a small bamboo cage until the war ended -if you lived. I felt certain I would rather be killed than captured, from what I had heard about being a POW with the Viet Cong.

"Next!" the supply sergeant called loudly to out the door for the next guy in line.

CHAPTER II: THE BLOOD OF LIUTENANT OAKS

"Hodgkinson," someone yelled into the barracks. I was still jet lagged from travelling halfway around the planet, just two weeks past. From Saigon to the replacement center in Long Bihn and now Dong Tam, it manifested into culture shock, or whatever they call it when you find yourself in a warzone from layback Northern California only two days before. The nonstop racket of chopper traffic, red alert sirens, exploding enemy mortars and rockets all around the base camp played hard on my nerves. I sat cross-legged on the thin mattress of my bunk, the rest of the several dozen beds in the barrack empty. "The whale, AKA the US Army has gulped me down, and I'm now in the dark underbelly called Dong Tam," I wrote to my girlfriend back home. I put down my pen and paper, the writing backboard a Times magazine.

"You on your lazy ass there inside, report to the airstrip, pronto!" someone yelled into the barracks door.

I wondered, where the hell is that? Instantly lacing my boots up, I dashed out of the building in a minute, and figured where I should go from the thud, thud, thud sound of a UH-1 rotor wash. I got there, at the end of the short airstrip in another minute. A guy wearing buck sergeant strips on a shoulder waved me to follow him. He didn't even bother with felicities when I arrived at his side. "Grab the other end of the stretcher," he demanded over the chopper noise. On the deck inside the opened door of the craft, upon a stretcher with wooden handles at both ends, lay a body-bag, clearly occupied by an adult. A full length of heavy-duty zipper closed the six some odd foot long olive-green bag. I took one end of the stretcher in both hands, helping the sergeant with the load. He lifted his end high, the stretcher tipping down at my end. I noticed liquid inside the bag, making a bulge in a wave rushing at me. At the end of the zipper gushed out, likely a gallon or more of blood, splashing onto me, soaking my shirt and pants all the way down to my boots. The blood was still warm from the person's freshly killed body. "What the hell?" I cried out.

The sergeant informed, "The crew chief of the medivac ID'ed him as Lieutenant Oaks, a platoon leader in Alpha Company. He said that the lieutenant took three or four bullets in the stomach. That's what the hell."

"That's my company that I've just been assigned to."

"How long you've been here?" He led the way with his end of the stretcher.

"I just arrived at Dong Tam the day before yesterday. I'm in holding pattern for the company to return from their mission, so I can join up with them."

"You just got here? And you've already been baptized in blood. Not just any blood, but the blood of an officer. An officer and a gentleman. That's an omen."

After a short time, we arrived at the field hospital, another unassuming plank structure, no paint or varnish. The sergeant reached with difficultly from the load with one hand, opening the door. We maneuvered the stretcher through the standard door size entrance. A hallway led in short way to a walk-in freezer. Awkwardly, the sergeant pulled open the heavy metal door at the end of the hall.

"Damn, where are the valets when you need them?" he swore. Once inside the air-conditioned room, the only people to greet us were dead, occupied body-bags stacked like cordwood atop one another. About a dozen of them. The sergeant and I dropped off our load known as Lieutenant Oaks atop a steel table. "I'll take notes from his wallet and give them to the company's XO, in route to the inbox of the chaplain to get off a telegram to his love ones back home, PDQ." He glanced to the pile of body-bags. "More of Alpha and Bravo company war heroes. I've already processed them. They're in queue for a ride back home in a refrigerated cargo plane. Those stiffs have been keeping me busy," his tone betraying little remorse. On the way back out of the building, the chaplain's assistant chatted. "This is what I do. I take bodies from the medivac choppers from the field, or from around the base camp after direct-hit rocket attacks and deliver them to the place we just left—officially designated the frigging morgue." As we walked towards the barracks where I was quartered, he spoke as if we had already become good friends. "Yeah, when I arrived In-Country seven months ago, I declared myself a conscientious-objector at the Army replacement center. So, they assigned my dumb ass to this job."

I chuckled. "At Advanced Infantry Training, in Fort Lewis, I told the company commander that I didn't want to shoot anyone, no matter their politics, religion or their dislike of anyone who doesn't have slanted eyes like themselves. I assured him I was a conscientious objector. The captain had a pleasant manner. Earlier in training, several IQ tests behind me, he had me report to his office, and offered to send me to Fort Benning to train to become a helicopter pilot. As he told me it would require me to sign up for an additional year in the army, I declined. I would be obligated to two tours in 'Nam. Anyway, he sat me down and explained that in such an event of becoming classified a conscientious objector, I would be assigned the MOS of a Chaplain's Assistant. There, I would take bodies from the field, tag them for identification, and finally load them into aluminum coffins for their flight back home. I replied I didn't know what I was I thinking.

"No one enlightened me as much as you were. Just saying Chaplain's Assistant sounds like you would be like an errand boy in some base camp chapel. I regret this fucking job every morning I wake up. Give me a rifle. I'll shot every gook who crosses his eyes at me."

"I'm not looking forward to that role in the footlights. Any time you want to trade jobs, let me know. I'll do all I can to get the paperwork cut..."

"You're kidding yourself. You just said that you went through advanced infantry training. All I did was basic at Fort Fantasyland Ord. When the slick drops you off in a rice paddy here in 'Nam, readily locked and loaded, you are a signed, stamped and delivered golden boy for boots on the ground in the Army. You will have a certificate from Reliable Academy here at Dong Tam. It's a weeklong jungle combat training school. Meanwhile, take note, that blood you're soaked is a sign. Not just a sign, it's a good sign. All-in-all, you just got your cherry popped."

I was beginning to feel annoyed with this preachy non-combatant, mainly in respect that he was telling me that I should appreciate the blood that had completely doused me. Perhaps he had something there -me just off the plane from pastoral Placer County, California. "Guess you've got my number," I somewhat deferred.

"You've got it. Numbers are what we're talking here. Ever heard of Chaldean Numerology?" he asked.

"Yeah, um, in fact that's my favorite type of numerology," I said in my best faked academic voice, being a wise ass.

A UH-I passed overhead. The sergeant waited until the clatter of the low flying craft abated into the distance. "Don't feel out of the loop. It's not a commonly known philosophy."

As we closed-in on the barracks, I couldn't wait to get inside and disrobe of my Baptized fatigues. I'll never forget the stench of Lieutenant Oaks' blood soaking my very skin pores. I planned to go back to the supply building the first thing in the morning and ask to be issued new fatigues. And this time, I would try them on right there to ensure they fit.

"In CO, becoming blood-soaked by fate, rates above all non life-threatening war experiences. That is what is called the winner mentality. It means you desire freedom and abundance. Your goal is to gain success, so you can do whatever you want in life. You don't need to get all wrapped around the axle trying to figure it out. It's predestined. You don't choose the course of your life; that flow of life chooses you," he informed me.

We were at the side door of the barracks. I didn't know what the hell he was talking about. A mosquito got me on the forearm, and I slapped it to death.

"I gotta get back to Earth," I exclaimed politely over the noise of the rotor-wash of a landing chopper nearby. I don't think he heard me. He just went on.

"A man fighting for his country is not by any concept a hired killer. A good warrior, with a cause, rates as among the best people on Earth."

"Yeah, fascinating." I had heard about all I wanted to from this blood-revering philosopher, who probably ranked Dracula among those he most admired.

The sergeant pointed to a quad of 4x4s supporting a plastic tank eight or ten feet high. "That's your shower. All you have to do is pull the cord, and *voilà* the water comes out. You can wash that blood off, but a Baptism doesn't go away. Holy water, blood, whatever." He bid me good night, never even giving me his name. The chest patch on his fatigue shirt, revealed to me that his last name was Johnson. I had to wonder if he had any relationship with that war criminal running the show in the White House. One thing for certain, I regarded, he needed a long vacation. Meanwhile, the sun had set an hour or so past, but it remained hot. I had no wristwatch anymore, having traded it with a Vietnamese housekeeper at the barracks in Long Bihn for a paper lunch bag of pot, which she called dinky dau. Anyway, who needs a watch in a warzone? If you're fifteen minutes late for a scheduled charge of a bunker, it's probably for the better.

I wasted no time going to the shower, stripping to the nude and washing myself in the lukewarm water. Someone had dropped a bar of soap on the metal grate at foot, and I made ample use of it. I lathered myself from head to toe with the half-used bar that scented of coconut. I showered for a long time, but the smell of blood would not banish from washing. I couldn't see it, but I felt that it was still there, absorbed into my very being. After fifteen or twenty minutes, the color of the blood washed away, but I wondered if I had really been Baptized, tainted in my opinion, by Lieutenant Oaks blood for all time—it might have well soaked to my bones. Maybe that Johnson character knew what he was talking about.

CHAPTER III: ALPHA COMPANY

In several days, Alpha Company arrived at the airstrip in a formation of nine UH-1s. Even though we were on the same side, those sweaty unshaven guys, bristling with weapons of every kind, and festooned with bandoleers of ammo clips, and grenades on their utility belts made me want to run for my life. Their boots and pant legs were heavily caked in mud. At the edge of the runway, a soldier gripped in both hands a large metal nozzle, the hose of which connected to a pump that drew water from the nearby muddy canal. Water under high pressure sprayed the troops, one at a time, cleaning them from waist down as they crossed in close rank towards the nearby barracks. You could look at their placid faces and tell that had just returned from Hell.

CHAPTER IV: INSTRUCTIONS TO SIDESTEP BOOBY TRAPS

Battalions sent me to Reliable Academy, just as the Chaplain's Assistant had foretold. I learned how to sidestep booby-traps along a jungle trail, how to detect a possible ambush, clever ways to set up your own ambush and everything you need to know, when you find yourself behind enemy lines. Did you know that you could make a fire with a pair of good eyeglasses, focusing the light of the sun on a small pile of dry twigs; or that water from a coconut, plentiful in the jungle, was a much healthier way to hydrate than drinking from your canteen, or that water buffalos often charge, horns full ahead at the GIs because they have a very keen sense of smell that warns them, we are hated carnivores? After a week of training, I was ready to launch.

Back at the barracks, the company was just back from their latest search and destroy mission. One of the guys, a fellow Californian from the town of Tahoe City named Easily, became a quick friend. He swept me off one night to the nearby enlisted club. At the entrance, a sign warned to check your weapon at door. No problem -we had left our M-16s at the barracks. The place was crowded, and music played loud. A group of four from Alpha Company waved us over to their table. We found two empty chairs and squeezed into the little remaining elbow space to join them. Easily introduced me to the others. A guy with a Southern accent, interrupted from speaking a second by our arrival, continued, "So my ol' lady gets back to the apartment from her waitress job, fetches a beer from the fridge, and joins me at the couch. She nearly falls out of her cushion, when I tell her I had signed up with the army to fight in Vietnam.

"Now, apropos, go to town and have *organ donor* tattooed on the bottom of your right foot," she coldly remarked.

Everyone laughed.

"I got a draft notice in the mail," a buck sergeant called Little John told. "That same day I had sold my old Buick for a good price," another guy recounted. "When my wife got back home from shopping, I told her, "I've got some bad news, and some good news."

"Oh, tell me," she replied while unpacking the groceries.

"Firstly, we're going to be separated for two years. I just joined up for the Army."

"Okay," she says. "And what's the bad news."

Us guys at the table had been swilling beer, telling such stories for several hours into the evening, when the red alert siren wailed. Chairs screeched across the wooden floor; several being knocked over with the mad rush for the only exit. I started to get up but noticed the guys at our remained seats were unfazed by all of the excitement. "For those of you who don't know, the bunker's just across the road," the bartender called loud. The place cleared out in a heartbeat. I looked to Easily and implored, "Aren't we going to the bunker?"

"And crowd in there with a bunch of sweating and hyperventilating REMPs?"

One of the guys at our table stood and began helping himself to beer from the abandoned tables around us, handing the opened cans out to us. Rockets exploded near and far as we drank and joked. Rocket here and there launched sight unseen from the dark jungle into the huge base camp. Some of the explosions were close. For anyone jaded from lots of combat, this presented nothing to get excited about -I was just learning.

The last week in June 1968 someone wakened me from my bunk to partake in my first mission.

"It's not even four," a skinny, blond kid complained after looking at his watch. "I thought I heard the lieutenant say we didn't have to get up until five."

"If you haven't noticed by now, we're on the Army's version of time and space," another guy put in with only a hint of humor in his tone.

"What the hell was I thinking?" the blond guy made a frustrated expression.

Meanwhile, the company commander took stance just outside the barracks, ordering his four platoon leaders to allow just fifteen minutes for the men to take breakfast in the nearby combat engineers mess-hall. Next, it was off to a metal shipping container, converted to a securely padlocked ammo-shed. Inside, it appeared Santa had come, and it was infantryman's Christmas. Along with the others, I had free rein to no limit of bandoleers of bullet clips, grenades, not to mention green, red and yellow smoke canisters -take your pick. After a flurry of pick and grab, like kids grabbing presents from under the Christmas tree only left behind were flak jackets in a large pile. I had been tempted to grab one but didn't for fear of appearing like a pussy to the other guys.

CHAPTER V: LOSING MY INNOCENCE

Nine Hueys lifted Alpha Company off, doors left open on both sides, for convenience of us firing back in event of a hot LZ and getting out fast. Destination, our commander informed, the Plain of Reeds, a monsoon-soaked agricultural region just south of Saigon. The low flying trip above a dense jungle that turned to flooded rice paddies, ended at last in a large area of pineapple plantations.

"Lock and load gentlemen. We're going in," our squad leader cried over the prop clatter. Indeed, we needed to lock and load. At around a hundred feet from setting down, bullets began riddling the chopper, holes appearing in the aluminum skin of the craft all around us. Those nearest the open two doors began firing their M-16s on full-automatic. As I sat on the deck next to the open door, vulnerable to the wood line below, I fired with a forefinger hard on the trigger. Even in the bright light of a cloudless morning, you could see the muzzle flashes of automatic weapons from the dense jungle. There were a lot of them, and those bullets were audibly whizzing and buzzing like angry bees to my left and right and just overhead. The door-gunner next to me fired his swivel-mounted M-60 nonstop, directing his barrel at a steep downward angle. After a minute, he slumped over his large weapon. It appeared he was dead. Our formation of choppers began to set down among hundreds of rows of early growth pineapples. The gunfire from the wood line became even more intense as we landed. So this is the dreaded hot LZ I've heard so much about, I marveled in comprehension of it all, as I hopped out of the chopper. I'm losing my cheery all over the place here, I tried to be lighthearted in thought. I joined the others with intent to charge the wood line, but the intensity of the enemy machine gun fire discouraged such plans. We all dropped prone in the mud almost at once and continued to return fire. Even with the roar of gunfire to both my sides, I could hear the company commander on the field radio nearby, calling in air-support. He gave his call sign and aspiring strike coordinates. "*Beaucoup* metal on the target would be much appreciated. Might want to mix in some napalm to show we mean business."

It didn't take long for the jets to arrive, doing warp speed from their base in Saigon.

After the airstrike, about a half-hour in progress, we were able to resume our charge. The enemy gunfire had ceased. All we found inside the wood line was a row of unoccupied well-constructed dirt bunkers. Only two of the dozen or so showed evidence of direct hits.

"Guess they all died," Easily concluded. All around were toppled coconut trees from the heavy bombing, several ablaze from the napalm. The blackened ground could be best described as scorched earth. The captain muttered, "Well, we did kill a lot of communist trees." At least he had a sense of humor.

Afterwards we spent the rest of the day in search of the enemy, recipient of just two snipers hit and misses, we found a good pick-up zone, and the six choppers took as passengers a gracious, and exhausted Alpha Company. But it wasn't over yet. Gunfire from the surrounding jungle began to pummel us as soon as we lifted off. Our airmobile ride took enough bullet hits in the motor housing, that the craft went into a spin and fell the short distance back to our pick-up zone. We hit the ground hard, but the skids absorbed most of the impact. "Everybody okay back there?" the co-pilot looked over his shoulder to inquire.

"My butt is bruised," said one of the guys.

"You'll get over it," someone else offered.

"And where'd you get your medical credentials?" the guy with the reputed bruised butt retorted.

"My back feels like a disk might have been crunched like a damned saltine cracker," someone cried. "But I'll live," he injected into the exchange.

"My back as well," I answered the co-pilot's headcount of those likely in need of medical attention. "I too expect to survive, unless the VC shoot us all, before we can get the hell out of Dodge."

"I really got to take a piss," came another retort. "Does that count?"

The co-pilot did not provide dignity by answering that guy. He only summed up, "I just want to know if I should radio in if we need a medivac. But from checking with you guys, I think we can get by with a passenger version of a slick to get us back to the base camp in one piece."

Meanwhile, all we crash survivors could do was to show that we meant business, firing into the jungle all around us, holding off the enemy until we were rescued. It didn't take more than a half an hour for the UH-1 ride to arrive, escorted by a pair of Huey gunships. The gunships blasted into oblivion every enemy hotspot our pilot had directed to them by radio. Us dozen infantrymen, plus the door-gunner, pilot and co-pilot were rescued in short time with no one getting shot, despite long minutes of exposure to much gunfire while switching crafts. The craft delivered us late-night back to Dong Tam. A medical officer had greeted us as we were disembarking. He announced that he had come there to escort any of us to the field hospital, who felt they needed care. Several others and I took him up on it. A field ambulance drove us the short distance. They subsequently X-rayed my back, in short, declaring me fit for duty within the next several days, giving me a bottle of pain pills and released me. I walked to my barracks nearby, very much wanting to sleep. Lights were out when I went in, and I walked quietly across the room not to wake anyone. Plopping down on the edge of my bunk, I began unstrapping my boots.

"Where've you been?" someone asked from the dark across the aisle between bunks. I knew it was Easily; the simple tone of voice in the dark is how well you get to know someone in a short time when serving alongside of them in combat.

"Saving the world from little guys in black PJs. Got shot down and surrounded by the enemy. We were rescued, but the crash hurt my back, and they X-rayed me at the field hospital. They just now released me as fit for duty." Once I took my boots off, I stripped down to my underwear and crawled into bed.

"Gad, a Hot LZ, a charge-the-bunker style assault of a wood line that came down to a firefight, and a back-injury results of being shot down -all in one day, on your first damned mission. You wouldn't be trying for a million-dollar wound by any chance?" Easily feigned his best to at least humor me.

"If that million-dollar wound, as you call it, is going to be at the expense of an arm and a leg, you can count me out."

"You FNGs don't know anything. A million-dollar wound is a manner of speaking. You get wounded just enough, but not too seriously, that the army discharges you, sending you home -for good. It's like you've won the lottery. That's what we call a million-dollar wound."

"Whatever," I replied. I had only been in-country several weeks, and I was already learning a whole new vocabulary. C-rations were rats, the field radio (transmission) operator was an RTO, jet pilots were zoomies, an M-16 was a Mattel, helicopters were slicks, the regular-army guys in the Mekong Delta were paddy humpers... The army often captured young Viet Cong and interred them in POW camps, clearly aware that they were a valuable boot-on-the-ground resource who knew their way around the jungle and spoke the local language -perfect as translators. They graduated after several months of intense indoctrination, were christened Kit Carson Scouts and assigned to US Army combat units. Now a million-dollar wound, was a term to further embellish my vocabulary. I fell hard to sleep, bromide being the sheer gravity of the day now behind me.

Along with the First Cavalry, One-hundred and Seventieth Air Transportation, was the same number designated our river transportation. These were Tango Boats. They were the very heavily armed riverboats left over from the Normandy Landing in WWII. These were serious watercraft -very serious craft. They were heavily armed, all thick metal crafts that were armed with four fifty caliber guns each, automatic mortar launchers, cut-off one-o-five caliber artillery piece that blasted beehive rounds to the shoreline to both sides of the craft to include at point a command boat that sprayed napalm, we called a Zippo. Each craft had a drop-ramp on front that carried around forty soldier each, was a half-dozen flotilla of a company or two of heavily armed infantry. They would hit the shore into the dense jungle, ramps quickly dropped, usually under heavy fire, men running from the bowl of the craft into the jungle shoreline, machine-guns firing on full-automatic. This place we arrived at this mission was called VC Island. It was a several miles long, half-mile wide island in the middle of the main course of the Mekong River -the place infested with VC- a major military stronghold. We ventured into the middle of the densely forested island. It comprised primarily of swampland. Our squad leader, Little John took the lead. A short Hispanic kid from Sacramento, he smoked pot on missions. That concerned me. I smoked pot all the time but felt certain I never would on a mission. When you're in the bush with the VC in ambush, to include their booby-traps on ever trail, the poisonous snakes, the brutal heat, on and on. You had to be at the top of your game. Little John had been on the frontline for around seven months. I had only recently learned that six months on the front line was considered rotation time for officers in the Ninth Division. In other words, an officer's so-called *shelf life* had reached expiration after six months, and he went on to a non-combatant assignment somewhere in-country for the remainder of his yearlong tour in 'Nam. Only a buck sergeant Little John was no officer. In my short time in a combat unit, I had witnessed that officers were the most likely to be killed, by percentage than the rest of us. That's because they were always front and center during battle. Also, snipers usually picked them out first. Sergeants were just behind in queue. Anyway, on this search and destroy outing in mid Sixty-eight, Fourth Platoon ventured out separate of mother ship Alpha Company per intelligence from the company's grilling of a captured VC. The sinewy Vietnamese man in black PJs informed of a large NVA weapons cache in the neighborhood. The company commander turned over the informant to our platoon. The Vietcong, just a local villager had been recruited by the NVA, he admitted to Tran our interpreter as if making excuse for being a VC. He led us down a narrow trail through the dense Mekong Delta jungle, to the cache. Little John kept a pistol at his back as he Indicated at a clearing saying to the interpreter that inside the nearby wood line would be the weapons cache. The platoon hung back on the trail, watching as Little John followed just behind the VC. Our company commander Colonel Marine took interest, and hovered overhead in his light observation chopper. An explosion tore through the quiet jungle recluse. I looked to see our squad leader falling, slightly launched in air from the explosion. The VC kid took off running, disappearing into the wood line. As Little John hit the ground on his side, another explosion happened. It became obvious that the VC had led his American captor into a minefield of booby-traps. John lay on the soil badly wounded. Our medic came forward, patching him up, with the help of one of our riflemen positioning his body to make it easier to get to his wound. After wrapping at least, a half dozen bandages on arm and leg on one side, the medic gave Little John a shot of morphine, as well giving him comfort by telling him that he would be okay, that our RTO had dispatched a medivac. John was bleeding badly from his numerous wounds, and he could bleed to death in short time. The RTO informed the colonel of the situation. Our company commander let the chopper down to the clearing. Afraid that the skids of the chopper my set off other booby-traps upon landing, the chopper hovered several feet above ground. "Load him aboard. I'll fly him to the field hospital in Dong Tam

Colonel Marine instructed on the radio to our RTO. It took three of us to lift Little John to the door of the hovering craft, trickily because of his wounds and the chopper wash making our load all the weightier, but we managed. In short time, the makeshift medivac promptly ascended off. As for the cache, we never found it, or recaptured the Viet Cong lodestone. Soon after, while on a subsequent patrol, the guy just in front of me during the squad's venture, dramatically fell to the ground - shot dead in his chest by a sniper unseen. The island in the middle of the main course of the Mekong River was only about a mile in length, and a sixth narrower, geographically small, but rendered itself very large in military regards, earning its moniker VC Island.

CHAPTER VI: THE RIVERBOATS AHOY

Everyplace, we were crossing provincial canals -narrow irrigation canals once dredged by the French up to a hundred years past. We got ambushed repeatedly. "Medic, medic!" you heard repeatedly. At dark, we made camp. A chopper flew in, picked up the wounded and dead, threw out extra ammo and rations and took off to the roar of heavy enemy gunfire from the bush. In Vietcong-Ville, if you were regaled for shooting down an American chopper, you were awarded a new bicycle, and a two-week R&R in Saigon.

We returned to Dong Tam by riverboat the next day, muddy and exhausted. So this is Vietnam, ten and a half months to go... I could barely comprehend.

Several bunks at the barracks had become empty from recent attrition. "That was nothing," Easily told me about the mission where Collins was shot in the head and killed right next to him in the U Mihn Forest –in English, *The Forest of Darkness.*"

"I've heard of the place." I replied reclining in my bunk. "Borders Cambodia, doesn't it?"

"Yeah, it's at the end of the Ho Chi Mihn Trail from Cam-fucking-bodia. It's freaking spooky all over the place. We go in there every three or four months, to collect Purple Hearts and Silver Stars. Bravo Company went in there early this year for a weeklong mission in company strength and came out in just platoon strength."

I only found out later from a visit to the small base camp library, after speaking to Easily, that during the First Indochina War, the U Minh

Forest became a Viet Mihn stronghold. In 1952, five-hundred French paratroopers dropped into what they then called the U-Ming Forest, to conquer the Communist Viet Minh. That entire force of French soldiers were never heard from again.

Upon the American occupation in the Sixties, that substantial piece of real estate populated into a well-armed Viet Cong and later NVA base.

"Do you know that Alpha Company, 3/60th 9th Infantry Division has earned the most Medals of Honor in the war in 'Nam. We're running the show dude." Easily was becoming a walking/talking source of trivia regarding Alpha Company's role in Vietnam.

"Thanks for the elucidation. I feel like I've ended up in the best outfit in the war." Meanwhile, I thought to myself, *Help me God!*

We were doing riverboats now. Our next mission would be to Mo Ci. The village was major Viet Cong-held territory. Charlie Company had set bivouac, a month past. They dug foxholes and settled down for several weeks or so. It's not like previous wars. Digging a foxhole in Vietnam is not such a good idea. For instance, in the two World Wars, the Germans dropped artillery day and night, and the American forces hunkered down in relative safety in their holes in the ground. The VC did not play by those rules. They simply laid low in the bush until the wee hours. They waited for the complacent Americans to fall asleep in their foxhole, and crawled up in silence, slipped down and sliced their neck with a knife while they were cat napping on duty. Charlie Company woke the next morning to find a dozen or more of their buddies' dead from cut throats.

Several weeks later, Alpha Company went in, and we set up a command post, called in artillery and air strikes, and in one evening blasted into moon strikes, with high explosives, napalm and white phosphorous the entire surroundings of the village. The VC was wiped out, along with all their coconut and papaya trees, their source of shade, vitamin C and B12.

We were endowed with a new captain. Captains had a shot shelf-life in our unit. Easily told me we had gone through six of them in his nine months in the Bush. They were rotated every six months because of their brief life expectancy. Several of them simply rotated out to admin jobs. The new captain had a good sense of humor. Just a few days in command, he introduced to the company his last name, and of course being Italian, he was a *dego* by slang. He made light of that term, joking about being a dego. He told us that in reference to Alpha Company, when the subject came up anywhere, "Where I go," he said, "dego."

We all politely laughed at his silly humor. Several days on his first mission we were in a clearing in some Mekong Delta outback. The captain was a bit lost. He had his map spread out in both hands, and all four RTOs surrounding, making calls, long antennas conspicuously sticking out overhead. A single shot rang out. The captain caught a single bullet in the forehead. He collapsed straight to the ground. A sniper picked him off. My instinct was to duck low to the ground in cover, but what would the sniper want with me after he just picked off the main man? He likely ran for his life into the jungle from the heavily armed company. We were ferried by riverboat back to Dong Tam for several days of rest. We would get a new captain within a week.

CHAPTER VII: DAWN IN THE DELTA

After two days of drinking warm beer and eating tasty hot mess hall food, we were back in the field. This time we were going to Bien Hoa. The LZ proved itself hot -very hot. From the air, several thousand feet above, Bien Hoa didn't look like such an unwelcome place -largely rice paddies surrounded by lush, coconut, papaya, mango and banana trees. At my side, our feet hanging out the opened door of UH-1, my charge accompanied me, an FNG just two weeks in the country. Shrader, an eighteen-year-old, hailed from a small town just south of Kansas City.

"If the LZ is hot, when we're around ten feet above ground, jump! Just follow me." I cried out loudly above the clatter of rotor blades just overhead. As the nine choppers of Alpha Company began to set down, bullets started making holes in the skin of the craft. I looked down. Large bullets, 51 caliber ones, began forming holes in the helicopter skids just beneath my dangling feet. The chopper formation found itself in the thick of it. When bullets, doing the speed of sound just past your head left and right, missing your head by a half an inch, they make a distinct crack. On full-automatic, it's crack, crack, crack. The gunfire from the wood line must have been from fifty or sixty, possibly a hundred bunkers. The door-gunner at my side was a favored target for the enemy, and taking numerous hits, fell dead over his M-60 on swivel-turret. Door-gunners in 'Nam have a two-month life expectancy. I don't know why anyone would take that job except a misinformed moron or someone suicidal. "Jump!" I yelled to my FNG. I did, in midair for several seconds with bullets flying all around me in my hurried freefall.

Seconds later, Shrader landed next to me where I stayed prone in the lightly flooded, thankfully soft rice paddy. Hundreds of bullets flew just above our heads. "Don't even stand up!" I yelled to him. We had at best visual cover from the foot and a half high rice stalk. "We'll just lie low until the choppers set down." In a minute, to my great dismay, it became apparent that was not to be. The fire from the wood line, about a hundred feet away, was so freaking heavy, the chopper pilots obviously feared setting down. They rather lifted skyward, and prudently flew off into the distance.

"Son-of-a-bitch!" I muttered. My FNG and I had just found out were now caught behind enemy lines. It seemed like perhaps a battalion of NVA Regulars, against two of us. Meanwhile, surrendering was not an option in my mind. Any form of being captured was not about to happen, I had decided from stories I had been told repeatedly after arriving to 'Nam. Becoming prisoner to the NVA regulars would mean torture, imprisonment in a small bamboo cage, starvation and likely a slow, miserable death after only giving your rank and serial number. I instructed Shrader to follow me in a low crawl to hopeful shelter. I felt certain the company would return after pounding the hell out of the wood line with artillery and airstrikes. We crawled through the paddy, deep in mud with our shouldered M-16s, for about a half an hour before coming to a rice farmer's hootch at the edge of the large paddy, opposite the enemy occupied wood line. The gunfire did not let up. Why didn't they just come out of hiding, and capture us? My guess is that they figured we were a couple of decoys, assigned to lure them out into the open, so our artillery could pick them off. No such mission existed. All I knew was to save my neck. I had Shrader follow me inside the wattle building. Here in the middle of all the shooting and bombing, all Vietnamese hooch's had their homemade bomb shelter in the middle of the living room. The homespun shelters usually consisted of several foot high, around five-foot-wide dried mud igloos. In the middle of the shelter a tunnel went into the earth. Underground was typically a dirt basement large enough for perhaps a Vietnamese family of five. I informed Shrader of this and told him that we needed to drop into the shelter for safety, until the company returned. We went inside the hootch. Sure enough found the igloo, and tried to go into it. Immediately came the distressed exclamations of a mamasan in Vietnamese, and the cries of children, perhaps three or four. I stepped back and looked at Shrader. "You know, they should have a neon sign here saying: *No ccupancy*."

We had no choice but to plop down in low profile, reclining against the wall of the indoor bomb shelter, opposite the direction of the leveled gunfire. It wasn't long before the American artillery arrived. Hundreds of high explosive rounds began exploding. You could hear them like a little freight train each, zooming their passage overhead, and greatly delivering their payloads into the wood line one after the next. Next came the jets. The ground shook. You could feel the shockwaves of heat from the napalm and white phosphorous explosions too close for comfort. "We're saved," I said in great relief to Shrader. He didn't answer. I glanced to see he was likely traumatized. I had been in combat long enough to recognize the signs in others. Just a month ago this kid, in a KC suburb, was sitting on a couch in his folks' home, watching the 'Nam played out and safely held in the confines of a TV screen. Those body counts Huntley and Brinkley tallied ever night, were now upfront and personal. Just a year younger than me at eighteen, he was not dealing with it -first the firepower of a battalion of NVA from hell raining down upon him; now something ten times more likely to knock your mental door leading to a secure dwelling place off its hinges, manifesting itself in form of God almighty American artillery and jet strikes, in your face.

I slapped a mosquito on my arm, then another one on my neck, and still another one buzzing around my ear. In less than an hour, the strikes stopped. Only minutes later, the sound of descending choppers lifted my hopes. I could hear clearly that there were nine of them I could pretty much tell from the sound. Alpha Company had returned.

"You gonna be okay to get up with me and run across that rice paddy in direction of those landing slicks?" I asked my FNG.

"I'm just scared."

"Well, at least we know your God-given instincts are well intact. Come on, let's get the hell outta Dodge." Shrader followed close behind as I lead the way out of our temporary residence and became an Olympic runner across the huge rice paddy. Just when you thought the world had become a safer place, it had not. Bullets instantly began kicking up the mud in little geysers at our heels -lots of them. Every thirty or forty feet came another dike and I lurch to my stomach beside it for cover for several seconds, would run again and repeat my down and up evasive tactics until arriving where the company had been dropped. The one-hundred and some odd men were lined up behind a long dike, returning fire into the wood line. I found a space at the dike among my fellow platoon members -Shrader at my side. He and I finally got to make use of our M-16s, firing on rock & roll into the woods until our barrels were too hot to touch. Hours rolled by into sundown, and the gun battle continued. All I could figure is those guys in the wood line must have brought a lot of ammo along. And they were apparently well dug in. Into the wee hours of the night, into the following morning, we finished off all our C-rations, drank all the water from our canteens and expended all of our ammo. On repeated calls to the choppers by Alpha Company by our commander for resupplies, the pilots were obviously afraid to come back in under such heavy fire. All we could do was hunker down behind cover of the dike and pray that we didn't get overrun. Our platoon leader had been constantly on the radio and passed on to us nearby him that he had good news. Bravo Company was soon coming in, reinforcements top-heavy with fresh ammo. Meanwhile, I had little to do with my time, so I rolled up my pant legs, and with a cigarette lighter, burned long, blood-filled leaches off my legs. They were even on my chest. When I heard the choppers coming in, my spirits lifted. I smiled to myself. I had a saying. Since the choppers were built by Bell Company, when they came to the rescue of us ground troops, I would always say in wordplay, "*Saved by the bell!*" The Fourth Platoon leader cupped his hand around a strobe light, in manner it could only be seen straight above. In their slow descent, the choppers began drawing heavy fire from the wood line. The door-gunners, two on each of the nine crafts had apparently mistaken Fourth Platoon for the enemy. They began firing their automatic weapons down at us. The men around me were being shot and killed one after another by our own men, the door-gunners. Shrader dropped to his side just inches away. I could tell he had been killed. By chance, I did not get hit by the hail of bullets. The choppers set down, and Bravo Company quickly offloaded under intense fire. They took up position behind the same length of rice paddy dike as Alpha Company. The choppers lifted off in a hurry, and disappeared into the night, NVA gunfire dogging their departure. When the sun rose the next morning, medivac choppers came in and carried away the wounded and dead. In military vernacular, what happened was called friendly fire. Some kind of *friendly*.

CHAPTER VIII: JOHNSON GOES AFTER HO CHI MINH

The big news was that by late 1968, American boys were getting killed wholesale. President Johnson wanted fifty-thousand soldiers a month for the war effort. But they were not available from military bases. So he tasked the U.S. Army to send National Guardsmen as replacements to Vietnam. The big problem is they were not trained for combat duty.

One hot muggy night, Alpha Company had set up for the night in a small jungle clearing, alongside a narrow provincial canal.

Never a dull moment. I became a swimmer with Fourth Platoon. I grew up an accomplished swimmer at a young age. When we moved around the Delta with its hundreds of provincial canals to cross, I always took my boots and shirt off and tie a rope to trees at either end of the canals. I fastened it well because the guys were weighed down with bandeliers of ammo and grenades. Part of my job was to carry the M-16s three or a four at a time above water, one hand on the rope. There was one guy I knew couldn't swim -Clements. I kept a careful eye on him as he crossed on the rope. He was a bit overweight, and with his ammo and grenade, in mid river I guessed that he couldn't hang on, and released the rope and went under. I dived in the water, found him at the bottom of the canal and swam him to surface. He was coughing water from his lungs. For the next several months, he stuck by me like a puppy dog. No doubt he loved me for saving his life.

Dredged for large areas of irrigation, and subsequent waterway routes by the French over a hundred years past, they crisscrossed the

Mekong Delta extensively in number and reach. Often shallow with mostly muddy shorelines, just the same, they were widely used as transportation routes between towns and villages by sampans, as there are few roads of any length, for vehicles in the tropical rain sodden ground and rice paddy flooded millions of acres of the Mekong Delta. Setting up ambush along a canal at night, ambushing with automatic weapons, often paid off well. If you shot-up a sampan or two loaded with ordinance, when they were without a escape option, they would usually explode and sink with all hands-onboard a duck shoot for certain. That was the case this September night in 1968. My platoon leader had put me in charge of a squad, awarding me with a Kit Carson 24/7.

"You just have to lay in wait, and you eventually hear the putt, putt, putt of the small engine coming down the canal," Tran assured me. He was right. About eleven or twelve, came the sound in the quiet night of the remote spot of jungle. A not very bright headlight shone on the front of the large sampan. It traveled in obvious stealth. We half-dozen, heavily armed troops lay in the prone at the canal's shoreline ready to open up with all we had. "Hold your fire a minute," I signaled with a fist held just above my head for attention. I heard a second boat close behind the first. We waited for the other sampan to come into view. In a minute, the two boats floated in the moonless night just before us. I raised that fist high and lowered my arm dramatically. We opened up at once. The roar of our gunfire erupted against the still, quiet night. The two sampans caught fire and began exploding. You became witness of the eerie images of men leaping desperately into the water with their clothes on fire. The explosion of ordinance threw some of them, cartoon-like from the two crafts. I lay there and watched the event unraveling. No combat resulted. To continue firing made no sense. We had caught the VC entirely by surprise, and they had no course of resistance. We laughed and cheered each other for a job well accomplished. Parts of burned wood craft and bodies eventually drifted down the canal. We camped there that night. I woke early the next morning feeling restless. I had powdered coffee from a packet from my rations. You could heat water from your canteen in a metal cup, over a chunk of C-4 explosive set aflame. There's nothing like a cup of powdered coffee and cream, early morning in the bush. But sitting there on the ground, the rest of the squad still asleep on their poncho-liners, a coconut tree trunk for my backrest, sipping my coffee, images of the people on fire, screaming jumping into the canal played vivid in my mind. Us squad members had cheered our massacre. How had I arrived so carefree, from the proclaimed conscientious objector before coming to this country, and now shooting people to death with great thrill? When we returned to the base camp for several days of stand-down, with Easily just behind, I climbed the one-hundred and some odd foot high communications tower, in the middle of Dong Tam. At top was a platform with just enough room for two people to sit. With the sky-high, 360-degree view of the military base, the surrounding dense jungle and the stretch of the Mekong to the immediate south, this was an excellent place to enjoy a joint. Coming back down the perpendicular, rail ladder while stoned, was another type of experience. Another cheap thrill was the spectacle of rocket attacks. In cadence with the red alert siren, rockets screamed past, loudly exploding when they hit in circles around us. Buildings in various parts of the base would splinter to pieces and burst into flames. Fire trucks and ambulances went racing in every direction. Later, if anyone was watching, they would have noticed two teenaged soldiers staggering as if from too much beer, headed down the dirt road that could take them from the communications tower back to their barracks. But we were not drunk, but rather stoned to the gourd on some excellent locally grown pot. I had purchased it from a village just outside the berm of the base camp. This village was well known as user-friendly to us GIs at Dong Tam. There you could get marijuana, rice wine and Ao Dai regaled teenage gals, you name it at commendable discount. As for the pot, just take your steel helmet off your head, turn it upside-down and a mamasan would fill it with leaves dripping with

THC, for just several piastres. The Vietnamese called their marijuana dinky-dau, meaning crazy plant.

As we managed our way back to the barracks, after the dust had settled from the latest rocket attack, I proclaimed, "That proved itself a real kick in the ass!" Easily readily agreed.

The next morning, the Alpha company commander came to our barracks and briefed us on our next mission. We were scheduled for airlift to a place named Can Tho early the next morning. This was the home base of the ARVN (Army Vietnam) IV Corps. The ARVN 21st Division had the responsibility of protecting the Mekong Delta's largest city of Can Tho. A big Problem, the South Vietnamese soldiers where not doing a very good job of it. The situation that Can Tho welcomed Viet Cong soldiers, as a place for their R&Rs, mixed company as much as it gets.

The battalion commander did not downplay the fact, in his brief that this wasn't just another search and destroy mission. Can Tho didn't rear it head simply as another battleground for us to address. We were going into a VC stronghold, only second to the Forest of Darkness in the Delta -I grasped the commander's undertones.

Our nine slicks, each one defying gravity, evident by high-pitched motor sound, about two-thousand pounds of troops and all their gear and weapons onboard lifted off from the patch of Dong Tam tarmac. In less than an hour, we landed in a clearing at the suburban outskirts of Can Tho. Suburban in the United States usually means rows of houses with two car garages on paved streets. This suburb generally comprised an occasional one room wattle structures, often alongside a muddy canal, with rice paddies for home gardens, and providing cash crop for living expenses. Why had us Americans come here in such force? Well, we were tasked to wiping out the VC in the surrounding areas of Can Tho, not the city proper. A large public relations issue got in the way. We gave it the euphemism collateral damages. With our awesome infantry firepower, in our support artillery and airstrikes, we were inadvertently killing a lot of women and children. Army Intelligence in Saigon had come up with a plan. We had separated civilians from the VC. The way we did that, with the help of paid Vietnamese laborers, the Army Engineers built hamlets all over rural Mekong Delta. These places were ringed by earthen berms, and bunkers all guarded by ARVNs. Civilians, mostly farmers, were rounded up and relocated to these hamlets. Now we could shoot up VC by the thousands, with little concern for collateral damage. We Christened this effort the Strategic Hamlet Program. After numerous day and night search and destroy ventures over the following week, to include some firefights, Alpha Company's commander cut us loose to visit downtown Can Tho on foot -something of a several days long, in country R&R. We could eat at restaurants, go to bars and screw lots of teenage pussy. We just had to keep our M-16s close hold, locked and loaded. Reason being that this city was sprawling enough to share itself as an R&R center with the VC. We could drink and dine alongside the enemy, in a hotel just across the street from one another, without incident within city limits for days at a time. All things considered, us always unwashed and muddy, machine gun toting jungle combatants, had something very much in common with the enemy. Like us, they were required to leave their weapons at their base camps when any of us were on vacation on R&R, none of use wanted to mix battle with pleasure. When you got down to it, VCs and NVA were more our ilk than the zoomies, the generals and all other REMPs back at the base camp. When we captured any of them, trained them as the recently affectingly named Kit Carson (a contractor for the U.S Amy), inviting them to join one of our combat units, they became among our best scouts. They knew the trails, the canal routes, the language and which villages were secretly VC /and or NVA. As for fellow enemy R&R vacationers, back in the bush, we were programmed to kill one-another.

CHAPTER IX: RELIGIOUS EXPERIENCE

Back in Dong Tam late one morning, I woke to the thunder of one explosion after the next. I listened for a minute and convinced myself to go back to sleep. It was only outgoing artillery. But the racket had fully awakened me. As Alpha Company had one more day of stand-down, I reasoned to myself I should make use of the time here at the base camp. I decided that I needed to confront the burgeoning beast inside me, before our next mission. We have a non-denominational chapel at the base camp, near the PX. I carried around a mental duffle bag crammed heavy with guilt, teenager naivety, questions all over the place about life, and foremost how can there be a God that lets wars like Vietnam even happen? I got dressed, cleaned-up and walked the hundred or so to chapel. Not being Sunday, the place was empty. There wasn't even a sky-pilot to be found. During the other six days of the week, the military occupants of Dong Tam had regular jobs. If there were infantry on stand-down, they were most often off to the clubs, the PX, massage parlors, barbershops or making use of the Olympic, above-ground swimming pool at the rec center. Inside, I did the ol' Catholic genuflex , made the sign of the cross, and took a seat at the aisle side of one of the rows of hardwood pews, close to the raised pulpit. The twenty-four-hour a day rush-hour of chopper traffic irritated me. The one good thing about the remote jungle during a mission was the absolute silence between machine gun fire. Here at the chapel, my initial thought, my very purpose here was to ask God to forgive me for killing others, not just killing them, but taking pleasure in doing so. I had not cracked open a Bible in years and strained my brain to remember relevant passages from its pages to validate my self-condemnation. Just then a man appeared from the altar. From his demeanor and high white collar, no doubt he was the minister. I kept my eyes on him as he descended the single step, and slowly approached me.

"I noticed you here all alone," he smiled. "Do you want someone to pray along with, or talk to –a shoulder perhaps?"

"Yeah, all of the above," I confessed. "I make a living out of killing people. I'm combat infantry... I'm not a good human." I felt my eyes becoming moist.

"I'm not sure where you're coming from," he looked a little sympathetic, but more misbegotten. "This is a warzone. It's kill or be killed if you are indeed an infantryman. When you shoot the enemy, it's in self-defense."

"Look, I was raised a good Christian," I retorted. "If there is anything I'm clear about it's that Killing is a sin. And you can't dispute the adage: *Thou shall not kill.*

"'Drink deep or taste not the Pierian Spring. Their shallow draughts intoxicate the brain and drinking deeply sobers us up again.' Do you know that adage?"

"Actually no," I admitted.

"Let's put it this way. I you're going to quote the Bible, know the passage of text you're quoting, not just a cut-and-save term here and there."

I had never met this character before, but from my first day in Dong Tam around three months past, I had a sampling of the mentality of his CO, the Chaldean Numerology guy. Explosions in near distance distracted my thoughts. Outgoing or incoming? -I wondered. The unsettling situation on ground at this land filled swamp turned base camp, was only second fiddle to my spiritual conflagration.

The minister had a Bible in hand and began a long process of flipping through its pages, quoting and commenting in his narrative. "There are many wars mentioned in the Bible. Wars of conquest (Joshua 1:6[1]), civil wars (Samuel 3:1[2]), and even a war in heaven (Revelation 12:7[3]). Of course, wars involve killing; there is no way around it. We know that murder is sin (Exodus 20:13[4]). But what about the killing of an enemy combatant during wartime? First, we know that not all killing in wartime is a sin. Get with the program! There have been times when God Himself commanded warfare." The minister ticked off each reference with a forefinger of his right hand, to a single digit at a time to his left hand. He looked softly at me. "You are not a bad person for shooting the enemy. Meanwhile, if you want to plea conscientious objector, put in the paperwork to your company XO, and if that request lands on my doorstep, I'll support you 100%."

I returned in a slow, thoughtful walk back to my barracks, slapping several mosquitoes along the way. I decided I would not be submitting any such paperwork that the minister had mentioned. I had a mental calendar like most of the guys. I had two-hundred and eight days left of my tour and decided to serve those days out on the frontline. I was one of the good guys. The sky rapidly darkened, and monsoon rains came pouring down heavily upon me. I hurried to get inside the barracks.

---

1. https://biblia.com/bible/esv/Josh%201.6

2. https://biblia.com/bible/esv/2%20Sam%203.1

3. https://biblia.com/bible/esv/Rev%2012.7

4. https://biblia.com/bible/esv/Exod%2020.13

CHAPTER X: SO-CALLED HAPPY HOUR

Several days later, back at Dong Tam over warm beer at the EM club, I expressed dismay to Easily about our last mission. "Can it get any worse?" I drowned my words with a quaff of Budweiser. The bar cranked up AFVN radio station, the song playing at that time was Lineman for the County sung by Glenn Campbell. His first-person character in the song lamented that he needed a vacation. Easily and I would listen to the song every time it came over the radio, and in a tacit agreement that a vacation would be in order.

"I've seen worse..." he responded to my dismay about the last mission.

"How's that?"

"It's called the U Mihn Forest."

"Pardon my Vietnamese..."

"The Forest of Darkness."

"I've heard mention of the place as being infested with NVA. On the Cambodian border, isn't it?"

"Yeah. It's at the end of the Ho Chi Minh Trail. It's very dense jungle covering a large area. It's a perfect hideout And it's a jealously protected resupply depot for all things weaponry, for years hauled on foot and bicycle from Hanoi to the Delta. During our last venture into that place, we found an underground hospital with even fricking ICU. Everything had been constructed underground. We found a motor-pool of motorcycles and jeeps in a handmade cavern! A ramp came out to above ground for easy drive out. Charlie Company went in there in late

'67. They went at company strength and came out at platoon strength. Nobody could say what happened to the rest of them. That place is scary."

"Wow," is all I could come up with.

"Oh, by the way, when you captured that VC and came into the base camp to deliver him to the POW camp, and got a day off, Clements went KIA." He told me this as if in passing. It was like that. I saved Clements life! He loved me. I knew that, and the feeling was mutual. We were connected for life.

Our command imposed upon us our next mission by riverboat transports. This flotilla of craft had the distinction of being monikered the 117th Mobile Riverine. They ferried us around the waterways of the Mekong Delta. Our main transportation was compliments the 1st Calvary, the 117th Air Mobility. It wasn't like us infantry had the luxury of just any old form of transportation. Early on at initial deployment of the 9th Infantry Division, we tried to get around dent of jeeps and armored personal carriers. It did not work out well. In the swampland known as the Mekong Delta, anything with tires or tracks bogged down hopelessly in the mud. You could venture a quarter of a mile on an attempted venture into a mission, and you ended up in mud up to your elbows. The so-called *tangos* were old landing craft left from the WWII landing at Normandy. They were the craft that carried fifty some odd infantry in their belly, make landfall, where at that point they dropped a ramp. The troops would clamber out into battle. These upgraded craft from the previous American war had become refitted for jungle warfare on a ship building island in the Pugent Sound of Washington State. They were not just troop-carrying landing craft. They were the exclusive way for us to get around in the huge swampland of the Mekong Delta, Destination Mo Ci. If you wanted to find a swarming beehive of the enemy, go to Mo Ci. The place was right there with Can Tho. Bravo Company had ventured there a month past. They had set up company headquarters in town. A perimeter of manned outposts went with their bivouac of several months. The guys dug in with foxholes around town.

What were they thinking? We don't do foxholes in the Delta. They just are not practical with the monsoon rains. And it isn't like WWII where it was a frontline, and your enemy had established a frontline. There were no battle lines here. It could be best described as a free-for-all. The VC crawled, around in the jungle, never being a target in the same place, and if we were smart enough, we crawled around in the jungle like them. Meanwhile, in just a night, a hole in the ground could fill with a foot of water, not just from rain but by virtue that the entire Mekong Delta is mud atop water. In Mo Ci, after only several days, fellow troops came around to look in on the company's outer perimeter guys.

They were all dead. Their throats had been slit in the night, while they had fallen asleep in their foxholes. Meanwhile Alpha Company was now going in to bust up the VC stronghold. The men of Alpha Company, by whatever providence, were elite warriors. Three medals of Honor were bestowed upon our company, the most by all counts, of any American military unit in that ten-year war. We were as bad ass as it gets, and no heavily fortified enemy machine gun bunker or two was safe from us. Watch out. Alpha Company is coming.

CHAPTER XI: CARPET BOMBING

We loaded aboard the riverboats at Dong Tam Basin, too damned early that November 1968 morning. Destination: Confront the enemy in South Vietnam swampland. In time and space, this was the height of the war in 'Nam. In no other period of the war befell a greater number of American deaths. We were getting hit hard. Meanwhile, what was the plan? The plan, according to 9th Division Command, was to take on the bad guys head-on. And us guys of Alpha Company were anxious to do so. The dozen riverboats, bottom heavy with ground troops churned their propellers in the murky waters of the Bassac branch of the river, eventually heading down a narrow tributary leading to Mo Ci. To get there, we would be going through a river intersection we called the Crossroads. We knew all about the Crossroads. In advance of us going through there, we had artillery pound the living hell out of the VC infested shorelines. As the riverboat propellers churned their way full ahead down the muddy channel, Huey gunships flanked us on both sides of the river. The gunships were as close as a helicopter could get to a jet fighter. Underneath each craft two rocket launchers were locked and loaded. And the choppers were fitted with fifty caliber mini guns. They ate VC bunkers for breakfast. Diving out of the sky like Ospreys going straight down after fish in a lake, their rockets scorched the earth in a long swath. Nothing on ground had safe harbor. Taking lead of the flotilla on the channel, we called the front boat a zippo, for loss of better moniker. The Brown Water Navy guys had fitted that craft with a cannon that spewed napalm. A continuous stream of napalm arched a hundred some odd feet, cremating everything along the shoreline. On each riverboat were four swivels mounted fifty caliber machine guns. And every boat came locked and loaded with a Holly grenade launcher, not to dismiss an eighty-one millimeters mortar tube ready to fire. But apparently, all that fearsome firepower wasn't enough. The VC knocked out the lead riverboat on this mission. That's all it took. When that boat got sunk, everything else stopped on the narrow waterway. The capsized boat backed up the river like a clogged drainpipe. B-40 rockets whizzed overhead. Several of them hit and exploded the riverboats sides. The boats turned quickly to shore and dropped their ramps. Us company of around a hundred infantrymen ran out of the boats with machine guns firing on full automatic. It wasn't even the start of battle. We charged through thick foliage, headfirst into dense jungle, the VC ambushed us, and numerous of us guys were dropping wounded and dead in battle. We threw hand grenades into their earthen bunkers that spit machine gun fire at us, and the roofs blew up high in dirt clogs, and men in black pajamas with AK-47s in hand fell forward out of their bunkers dead. Another day in the Delta. I had been on the front line for seven months, and I needed a break. I knew that I had earned one.

Not long after the Mo Ci mission, we gained support from the B52Fs. All we had to do was give them grid coordinates for any area of heavy VC controlled real estate. They did the rest. A five square mile area of target would come under what we referred to as carpet bombing. The riverboats carried a regiment of infantry, the $3^{rd}/60^{th}$ into the fighting theater. That consisted of the strength of four infantry companies. The B-52 Stratofortress were hardwired, among other bombing missions, to provide close air support to combat operations in Vietnam. Meanwhile, we were user-friendly to a fault. Prior to a bombing of that five square mile area, small planes dropped leaflets warning that in near future there would be a mother-of-all bombing, and innocent people should seek shelter, preferably get the hell out of town for the next several days.

The riverboats brought us infantry up the Mekong River close into the area of interest the day of the planned bombing, just hours before the arc light event, everything was carefully coordinated. Of course, the VC would take heed of the leaflets we dropped. Our plan would be to catch them on the run, our weapons all locked and loaded, our visual on high alert. We waited afloat in the river during the bombardment, so close to ground/zero that the surface of the several hundred-yard wide river swished from one bank to the next, like the waters at high sea during a storm. From a distance, we must have appeared like rubber ducks in a bathtub. Once the bombing finished and the waters calmed, we made for land. The brown water men lowered the ramps, and us heavily armed infantry clamored out of the hull. As it turned out, we could save our ammo. No VC, as we expected were there to defend the shoreline. As we ventured into the area that had been bombed, it looked unbelievably devastated. The jungle had been reduced to coleslaw for miles around. Nothing moved.

Starting in 1965, to nearly the end of the war the United States conducted *Operation Arc Light*. This was deployment of B-52F Stratofortresses from various US bases to conduct significant strikes upon enemy bases, supply routes as well as close air support to combat ground operation in Vietnam.

The commander of 3/60th Battalion, 9th Division, Colonel Marine got an idea in mid-December 1968. We needed to fight the enemy in direct kind. He would experiment with my platoon, the heavy gun guys, 4th Platoon, 3rd/60th. He regaled us *Ranger Six*. Us 13 guys, at current strength, would be choppered in, without lights, at the end of the Ho Chi Mien Trail late night. And it didn't matter how many rifles, pistols, or grenades we carried on hand. The main thing is, we had radio communication for rapid fire support with artillery emplacements for all over the Delta. If we saw even one VC holding an Ak-47 in hand, we could call in a marking round --a star round and ID exactly where we would bring in dozens of high explosives. My assistant Russ and I had a map of the area, and a flashlight in the dark. We knew how to determine the exact grid coordinates. Better yet, we would light up the entire overhead sky with parachute flares. We were so good with our map, compass and felt pen circles, doing the longitude and latitude, we would bring in the artillery within twenty feet by inches from the place where we hunkered down. And when we killed all the VC, and brought down coconut and mango trees around us, our platoon leader called in a slick and we got the hell out of Dodge, back to Dong Tam for several days of stand-down, until the next freaking, crazy mission. Ranger-Six turned out to be a very bad idea. The missions were too high risk and got most of us wounded and killed. But Colonel Marine, flying overhead in his light observation chopper was totally in his element. I'm certain he felt proud of his brave troops, under his command, sacrificing their lives for God and country.

CHAPTER XII: THE FOREST OF DARKNESS

Dong Tam, the EM club, early January 1969. Over beer, Easily became loose lipped and told me the top-secret news that he overheard from our platoon leader, Lieutenant Young. In two days, 4th Platoon was venturing into The Forest of Darkness. It was so secret, that the U.S. Army didn't want the VC, the NVA and the snoopy American media to know that we dared to venture, against international agreement, into Cambodia to shoot the hell out of anyone trying to cross the border carrying loads of weapons into 'Nam. All the sad news aside, us dozen or so guys were a major implication. It was not our strength in number as before mentioned, it was our war skills. We had it down to a science to spot the enemy and bring in the wrath the American artillery, and air strikes with napalm and white phosphorous all over the damned place. 4th Platoon was ferried up the Mekong River at night in a riverboat escorted by two other heavily armed boats, one in front, the other in back. The boats traveled slowly to keep their diesel engines as quiet as possible. Russ and I were checking our map twice in the hull of the riverboat, making certain we had our grid coordinates right, before we were dropped off. Serious business confronted us. After about seven hours of travel, the boat turned to shore, the Brown Water Navy guys quickly lowered the ramp, and unloaded us, like we had just made valet parking at the Holiday Inn. The jungle of the U Mihn Forest has very dense vegetation. We had expected it, and several of the guys wielded long sharpened machetes and chopped away bamboos and sugar cane, banana trees, you name it, and made us a clear path. Even at this late hour of night, we could see our way well from the starlight that is ever bright in the clean air of the Mekong Delta -that is, when it's not cloudy or raining. It was getting routine, our fifth or sixth mission into the Forest of Darkness. We became good at it. In time, we found a stretch of trail. You could tell of frequent foot travel from the compacted earth and the width of the passage. Such location would usually prove a good ambush site. We had been in battle long enough to know, all we had to do was not smoke or talk so as to not give ourselves away. And once you took your position, you didn't want to move around and rustle the bush around you. We waited in complete silence, often for hours. But they eventually came along, bearing lots of rifles, pounds of ammo in canvas bags and supplies of every kind. Some came on bicycles. We usually had before us a duck shoot, because these skinny little guys were so weighed down on their backs with rucksacks of supplies. The best bet was to call in artillery, and to get it over quick. That way, we wouldn't get too badly shot up. Russ and I did the coordinates, called in by field phone a starburst, a marking round, and with that assuring accredit ground/zero, called in fire for effect. Sometimes we called in flares, if nothing else, to give light to the darkness that was the advantage to the Viet Cong. The flares came down from the sky in tiny parachutes, lighting up everything almost as bright as daylight. If the enemy was going to charge us from the bush in large numbers, at least we could see them by light of flares.

The heavy assault of artillery had already done their job. Next, we called in a chopper to go back to Dong Tam. Well, it turned out we had been too confident. Apparently the NVA became very upset about us American's treading on their sacred U Minh Forest and bringing in artillery on their heads. They had established themselves there with a huge underground hospital; they had jeeps and motorcycles hidden underground with dirt ramps to drive out. We went into battle after battle. But us American were wasting our time. They were dug-in deep, and not going anywhere.

CHAPTER XIII: A FISH IN HONG KONG

February 1969 - R&R. When I arrived in Hong Kong, and after settling in my room for a two week stay, I went down to a small nightclub on a street in Kowloon. The prettiest girl I've ever seen approached me while I was having a beer. A sixteen-year-old at best, she slinked sexy like a pro up to me. That obvious discredit aside, she looked delicious to this nineteen-year-old kid. I bought her a tea for three times the price of my beer, and she came-on to me strongly. She told me her name was Helen Chow. By around eight or nine, I asked her if she knew a good place to eat. Helen offered to join me in a place nearby, but I declined. She suggested that I might want to jump on the Star Ferry and get a meal at Victoria Island, only a short distance away. I boarded the ferryboat. Thanks to a taxi driver on the Victoria side, I was taken to a well-furnished whorehouse with flowery wallpaper, where a madam presented girls for me to choose. I found one out of the lineup, and the madam asked a certain amount from me to take the girl to my hotel room, and I peeled out two twenties from my wallet and paid her. Meanwhile, I told the girl I wanted to eat before going to the room, and she took me to a restaurant nearby. We were seated at a long table, with around a dozen empty chairs. As we took our seats, the chairs began to fill up with all the girls from the lineup at the whorehouse. I felt flattered to become surrounded by all the pretty young girls. They all spoke in Chinese among themselves, but when addressing me, deferred to English with a British accent. They ordered white wine, ate expensive meals into the evening, and finished off with dessert. The waiter came at the end of the pig fest and handed me a bill for the whole bunch of them. I took the surprise of ruse in stride, a bungling fathead from out of town the first night in Hong Kong. After eating and drinking to their limit, the girls staggered out, several at a time on their way. I reluctantly paid the huge bill. The young Chinese girl and I eventually took a cab to the wharf to catch the Star Ferry to Kowloon. As I started to get out of the car at the wharf, the girl said, "Forty dollars please."

"What?" I blurted.

"You have to give me forty dollars to go to the hotel with you tonight," she demanded.

"I already paid forty dollars for you."

"That was to the madam. Now you have to pay me."

I got out of the cab, went to the driver's door, handed the man a fiver and told him to take the girl anywhere she wanted to go. I waited for only a short time to catch the ferry back to Kowloon. I arrived down the empty sidewalk to my hotel around midnight. Just behind me, as I walked, I overheard the sound of high heels on the cement coming up fast. I looked over my shoulder. "Hello there army guy," the young Chinese girl said. I recognized her as the girl I met in the street side bar below my motel when I first got to town. "Go away," I muttered.

"Why you saying that to me?" she sputtered. "Don't you remember me from earlier today at the club?"

"Yes, I do. Another Chinese bar-girl." I continued walking without looking back. She hurried to come alongside of me.

"What, you no like Chinese bar-girls?"

I glanced to her at my right side, and slowed my pace, as she was having a hard time keeping up with me. "I've only been in Hong Kong one day and have already been ripped off by every girl in town. I went to the Victoria side, per your advice earlier, and the whole bunch of them took me for a ride. I came to town with five-hundred dollars this morning. Now I only have three-hundred and fifty left. I paid the hotel in advance, but I still need to eat. And I want to sightsee around your beautiful city, but I don't think I can afford the remaining two weeks here -not at this rate."

She chuckled. "You're a fish. You swam right into their net."

"A fish? A fish! That's the way you people regard me when I come here as a guest from another county?"

"Too bad. Welcome to money hungry Hong Kong."

"You're cold hearted, aren't you?"

She chuckled again. "Your problem is, you let people take advantage of you, because you aren't smart about money. I think I'm going to have to take care of you while you are here in Hong Kong." We arrived at the glass doors of the hotel lobby.

"You want to come to my room with me?" I knew she was a working-girl but had little problem with that. Hell, I sleep all around the place for free of charge -who am I to judge, I considered.

"Of course, I will," she said. "I liked you very, very much when I met you first."

We made love in the hotel room. The radio on the bedside table began to play Live for Today by the Grass Roots. Helen remarked that it was her favorite song. "Mine too," I told her almost ecstatic at the coincidence. She started singing along, passion in her tone. I conked out, a casualty to jetlag from my Saigon to Hong Kong trip. Helen woke me for lunch in late morning. She knew the best dining venues downtown and took me to one nearby. We looked good together -she knew it and I did too. We drank oolong tea with cream, and I ate delectable Chinese food with the zest of a kid who had been living in the jungle on C-rations for eight months. Helen watched me with obvious amusement. I barely could get the stir-fry in my mouth with chopsticks -no silverware available at the table. After the meal, I had a Singha Lager to wash everything down. Helen broke the news to me of her plan. "You've got Three-hundred and fifty left?"

I took out my wallet and counted. "Three-seventy-four."

"You give me three-hundred and fifty and keep the rest for beer and cigars, or whatever. I'll take the rest of the money and support you while you're here. I'll show you around town to all the best places, we'll go the top of Mount Victoria, to the best restaurants, dancing at the clubs, and have lots of sex." She held a palm out across the table.

"Sounds like a plan." I could hardly believe my luck. I stacked the bills into her palm. In the following days, Helen lived up to her words. She handed me Hong Kong on a silver plate. We crisscrossed the town by rickshaw. She even took me to her parents' apartment in town, and proudly introduced me as her boyfriend. She took me to her bedroom in the apartment and showed me a small stash of gold. A future dowery? I felt honored. By the end of my stay in Hong Kong, having an intimate last meal at the airport with Helen, I implored her to come to America and marry me. She blushed and answered that she would.

"I want to see the Tower of Big Ben in person," she revealed.

I didn't have the heart to tell her the fact of Big Ben's actual location.

When I returned to Dong Tam, one of the guys from Alpha Company greeted me as soon as I jumped out of the truck from Saigon in front of the headquarters building. He had some bad news for me. I did not have a platoon to return to. In my two-week absence, most of the guys in 4thPlatoon were wounded and killed from an artillery round booby-trap. Only several of the guys were unharmed, he told me. I dropped in on the field hospital to see Jimmy Rogers, the guy who had been walking point and triggered the booby trap that took out the platoon. Ironically, he survived, but was missing both legs from the thighs down. As his squad leader, two weeks past, I repeatedly cautioned him to walk point-flank. This meant not to walk in the middle of the trail, but rather alongside of it to avoid booby traps. He ignored my warnings. While I was in Hong Kong, he bungled down the middle of a trail. Now, heavily sedated on morphine, his voice slurred, at least his spirit sounded positive. He told me the doctor told him that he would receive a generous disability compensation from the army for life. Jimmy was only about nineteen, my age. He planned on buying a gas station when he returned to his hometown in Ohio, he told me. I glanced to the sheet where his legs ended beneath. I found it extremely troubling to see what happened to him, especially in such youth as myself. Next to Jimmy's bed was a kid with a missing leg, he had been listening to us talk. This was the amputation area of the hospital.

"What happened to you?" I asked. He pointed a thumb to the bed on the other side of him, to a kid asleep, both legs missing. "That son-of-a-bitch stepped on a booby trap, and I was right behind him."

CHAPTER XIV: THE PUNJI PIT THAT SAVED ME

In around a month, the battalion began rebuilding 4th Platoon with poorly trained National Guardsmen. Most of them were reluctant to go into battle. In combat, your life depends on each other's soldier skills and their bravery. I saw little of this among this pack of new guys. I understood that they were drafted National Guardsmen with training mostly for stateside duty, such as riot control, but I had little use for them.

Several months after my return from Hong Kong, while on a mission I was walking point flank, the ground went out from under me and I went down. I had fallen straight down into a six-foot deep punji pit. At the moment my boots hit the ground, I heard a large explosion. Dirt clogs and shrapnel flew just over my head. I heard someone cry, "Medic!" The pungent smell of cordite permeated the air. Shouldering my rifle by the strap, and pulling myself out of the hole, I took account. Inside the punji pit were numerous upright bamboo stakes coming to sharp points at top. These were meant to impale the victim -the spear tips usually poisoned. Fortunately, my jungle boots had separated the stakes as I fell in with no injury. And how about the explosion? On my hands and knees, I turned my attention to the nearby trail. Three bloodied men were laying in the middle of the jungle footpath. The medic was attending to them with the help of others in the platoon. It appeared obvious that the point man, an FNG national guardsman had stepped on a booby trap. One of his legs was badly mangled. As I had been walking alongside the point man, just off the trail, my timing of falling into the punji pit was serendipitous. I had fallen to safely beneath ground, only seconds before the explosion.

CHAPTER XV: MY REPLACEMENT

Since I had been trained for heavy weapons at Fort Lewis, I requested our first sergeant, who ran our admin, for a transfer to the mortar emplacement in Dong Tam. Knowing me well enough to understand that I had used up eight of my proverbial nine lives, he said he could make it happen, with the caveat that he would have to first find a replacement for me. Alas, 4th Platoon suffered a serious manpower deficit. Us guys were being killed and wounded faster than we could be replaced. FNGs made it worse. Upon a new kid, fresh out of Reliable Academy with commendations, befell my escape plan. Our platoon leader told me I had been cleared by battalion to transfer to the mortar emplacement in Dong Tam in three days.

Frank Fabian, from Chicago impressed me as someone worthy of being my replacement. In Dong Tam during a stand-down, I spent day and night with him with the knowledge he would fill my space. After nine months in the bush, most of my platoon killed or badly wounded, I was a pretty good mentor. I told him, especially if he was on point, not to walk down the middle of the trail because of the booby traps. Walk point flank, meaning to walk alongside the trail, at least slightly out of harm's way. My knowledge of this precaution came firsthand/ up close and personal. Don't remain standing during a firefight. It's not cowardly to fall to your knees or to the prone when bullets start flying from the bush -it's good sense. You do want to return home one day, don't you? Have two canteens of water on your utility belt for every mission. If Charlie doesn't get you, the Mekong Delta heat will. As you venture out on missions, walking through villages and among rice paddy farmers, be polite. You have the automatic weapon and hand grenades; they only have their deference in return. In Vietnam, deference is not a weakness; culturally it's their way of being polite and agreeable to others. Show mutual respect. You know the villagers flip flop between support of us Americans and the VC has a lot to do with our good or bad table manners. Us Americans tend to be harsh and overbearing every way in behavior. The Vietnamese are forgiving and gentle people by nature. In gatherings, such as at a restaurant get together, they speak quietly, their body language is always polite in respect to others around them. Us Americans must appear like Neanderthals with our loud, bungling behavior.

I could tell that Frank absorbed my lecture completely by the way he intently listened. After the fact, I realized I should have told him more about the unwritten, hands-on survival in the bush -such as placement of the claymore mine. When you set up the mine on its two small tripods, you should place a hand grenade underneath, weighing it down with the heavy explosive device. Finally, you pull the pin from the grenade. In the event that the VC crawl up at night and turn the anti-personnel mine around on you, as it is a common tactic. When they lift the claymore, the grenade explodes and sets off the highly explosive device -to the elimination of one more Viet Cong.

Frank Fabian discovered the hard way that the above ground mine blasts metal balls dozens of meters like a large caliber shotgun.

CHAPTER XVI: THE MORTAR BARGES

The mortar emplacement presided over the far western side of the base camp, consisting of four tubes on two barges docked at Dong Tam Basin. In the middle of each barge a steel building had been welded nicely in place with bunks, safe from bullets and shrapnel inside. The barges were tied with large ropes from each barge to poles dug deep on shore. Long wood planks made ramps providing access to terra firma. The barges were just several hundred yards from Dong Tam's huge ammo dump, storage place of tens of millions of dollars' worth of all sorts of ordinance. The term dump didn't do justice to the fact that this real estate, inch for square inch housed in hundreds of sandbagged igloos, our most valuable of assets of bullets, grenades and high explosive artillery rounds, this being a military base in the middle of enemy territory. Our closest non munition neighbors were the barracks for the army musicians, which turned out to be serendipitous for us mortar guys, as they had one of the best mess halls on the base, and that's where we got to eat. An additional treat was the musicians showed movies on a large screen outdoors on weekend nights. Being a non-combatant wasn't such a bad thing after all, I considered. But our twelve mortar men were still infantry, and when rockets and mortars began striking the base camp, we had to rush into harm's way and man our guns, firing what we called counter mortar until we beat off the assault. This was a job that usually kept us up all night, as this was when the VC pounded the base camp hardest.

CHAPTER XVII: A MILLION GALLONS OF JET FUEL

Just down the road from the musicians' compound were two five-hundred-thousand-gallon storage tanks full of jet fuel. They were huge tanks, but unassuming, rusty and more industrial than military in appearance. That perception changed for me dramatically one evening in January of 1969. I was firing mortars in what we called harassing fire as we did every evening, unpredictably into the night. This involved randomly lobbing numerous rounds just outside the perimeter of the base camp to discourage Charlie from trying to over-run us. As I lifted one of heavy rounds to drop into the tube, one large explosion followed by another, sent concussions with force enough to knock me off my feet. The mortar rounds are attached at the bottom with powerful nitro charges to launch them from the tube. All I could think while falling backwards was to keep the charges from hitting the metal deck and exploding in my hands. I landed hard on my back, the twenty-pound round crashed safely to the cushion of my chest. My back wasn't so lucky. After a minute, I returned to my feet to see the two fuel tanks consumed with fire, each with a B-40 rocket hole in each. Fire engines soon arrived, but it took hours to douse the flames.

One of the guys from 4th Platoon dropped by the mortar emplacement for a visit. He bad news. My replacement, Frank Fabian had been badly wounded. He said that on an overnight mission, Frank had strung out the electrical detonation cord to his claymore mine about thirty or forty feet from his position. He sat down on the ground with his legs crossed, on guard duty for the platoon. Likely he heard the sound of bushes being shaken in the dark night. Frank hit the trigger to set off his remote detonated claymore. The whole thing had been a carnival-level trick on him. The VC had crawled up in the night and turned the claymore mine around and made noise with the bushes. The device ended up exploding on Frank.

CHAPTER XVIII: THE NIGHT THE AMMO DUMP BLEW

I visited the EM Club one Friday night in March 1969 with another guy from the mortar emplacement. At the club we were entertained by three pretty dancing girls from Michigan -a USO sponsored group, with a live rock and roll band as compliment. Us GIs serving in 'Nam referred to American girls as round-eyes. They were superior to the Asian females. Despite the beauty of Vietnamese girls, the round-eye ones were the girls we longed to return home to and marry. I had little interest in drinking the warm canned beer while watching the girls dance. When I got back to the mortar emplacement late that evening, all I could do was rattle on to the others in reference to the three young dancing girls from Michigan. The guys who had not gone to the club that night, missed something special. Later, that same night came an explosion so large, that an incredible flash of light preceded, with the concussion, our barge swishing in the water. The explosion came from the area of the ammo dump. Outdoors with other members of the mortar emplacement, sitting around smoking pot and hashes from a hookah pipe, a concussion and hot air blasted us.

"Man your guns!" our platoon leader yelled. We all scrabbled, setting up our firing direction to just beyond the berm to the west of the ammo dump. This is where we suspected the VC were lobbing mortars into the ammo dump. We fired all four guns repeatedly until our ammo was exhausted. The ammo dump went up again, this time in an explosion so great the ground shook three times as much as from the initial explosion. If you looked in the moonlit sky, you could see thousands of black specks high above. Those specks became larger and larger. It turned out the specks were chunks of exploded ordinance. One of those chunks came down and hit the gun barrel I had been firing -the metal so hot it glowed in the night. The fifteen or twenty-pound piece of metal ricocheted off the gun barrel and just missed hitting me as it flew by. I held my last mortar round in hand, nitro charges set it to the floor of the deck. Many more chunks of metal were falling from the sky all around, hitting the barges and splashing into the water. I had seen enough and yelled, "Abandon ship!" No-one hesitated. The two barges emptied out in seconds. The guys ran down the two ramps and the guy in front no doubt felt the rain culvert, under the nearby dirt road, would make a good bomb shelter and crawled into it. The rest of the dozen or so guys followed, all disappearing into the several foot diameters under road drainage pipe. The guys ran past me, and I ended up last in the rush. When I got to the end of the culvert, someone's pair of combat boots were sticking out, and it became obvious the culvert, crammed full could not accommodate anyone else. Ordinance was still raining in pieces -an up to basketball sized grey metal chunks hailstorm. I needed shelter and knew the musicians had their own bunker. I ran across the dirt road to that compound, and straight to their bunker only a few, pumping heartbeats away. Inside the sandbag shelter, a dozen or more musicians were hunkered down. Among them, I noticed above and beyond the musicians, were the three dancing girls from Michigan, who I had earlier grooved upon at the EM club. I ascertained then that that they were being quartered at the musician's compound and had taken refuge in the above ground bunker when the ammo dump went off. Outside, the ordinance at the dump continued to cook off into the night. Explosions continued for hour after endless hour. The bleached from too much reality, frozen faces of the three girls be-told that they were above and beyond equals in shock. In role by chance, a readily available, apropos expert while you are under military siege, as the only infantryman in the bunker, I felt a responsibility to comfort them -but what was I going to say? Everything's going to be alright, when I didn't even believe that. I just sat there, cross-legged on the dirt floor of the bunker listening to the carnage of repeated explosions. Would opium-fueled hordes of VC now overrun the base camp, AK-47s shooting on full-automatic at everyone still alive? A thud reported several feet above, and dirt from the sandbags on the roof of the bunker came down in thin cascades between the overhead timbers. "That was a direct hit," one of the musicians, in a near panicked voice assured those closest to him. Another loud thud struck home, followed by a stream of dirt. "That was also a direct hit," he continued to keep track. Thank God, the roof of the bunker did not collapse on our heads, and we did not get overrun, and at sun-up, the explosions stopped. We straggled out of the bunker, one at a time, mere survivors of a long night of a relentless hailstorm of chunks of exploded ordnance. Everyone appeared traumatized, but my heart especially went out to the three girls, because they were so unprepared for the event of the ammo dump explosion. They, of course, had no military training to aid in tempering that experience. I learned several days later that the girls had all been killed in an ambush of the jeep they were riding back to Saigon to catch a flight home to Michigan. Meanwhile, everything just kept getting worse at Dong Tam base camp.

I went by the field evacuation hospital nearby to look in on Frank Fabian. He was on morphine but able to convey to me that he took a lot of shrapnel in his midriff. Some of it was embedded in his liver and kidneys and could not be removed. The good news he would soon be flown back to a hospital in the United States.

Relieved from frontline duty, to serve at the base camp became much less the blessing I had expected. Dong Tam had become nicknamed *rocket city*. We were increasingly and constantly getting pounded with 122 and 244-millimeter rockets. The VC and most prominently the NVA had surrounded and zeroed in on Dong Tam base camp. You could not sleep at night from the red alerts. Sirens became constantly going off at the cadence of exploding incoming.

CHAPTER XIX: WALKING TALKING PEACE

Henry Kissinger came more prominently into the scene. Ironically, Nixon notoriously anti-semitic, embraced this guy as his greatest ally. And Nixon had a huge problem with the war in Vietnam. It divided the United States, and badly tarnished our image around the world. Protesters were surrounding the White House. They were crawling all over the place. They had come to town from such places as California, Iowa and New York by the thousands, and were blocking the Memorial and Key Bridge from traffic movement. They had taken over Washington by sheer numbers. Nixon downed probably four or five gin tonics -his favorite social lubricant, left the White House sans security, and walked over to the nearby Lincoln Memorial, the place of the main number of people at the end of the end of the Gathering Pool. And he announced to the crowd that he had come there to ask forgiveness. He stood there in repose, as the greatest man on Earth, making this offer to the people, mostly out of towners, and disenfranchised students from Georgetown and other nearby universities. They hated Nixon. They chanted a mantra, don't give-up the screw, vote Dick Nixon out in '72. A real bastard, Nixon arbitrarily threw young American men at Vietnam, and they were getting killed by the thousands. Those gathered by the Lincoln Memorial did not want to forgive him. They rather booed and berated him.

At a January 1969 meeting of the National Security Council, the General Commander of the Military Assistant Command Vietnam, stated that the ARVNs had been steadily improving, to the point at which the war could be "de-Americanized." This term would be fit into the broader détente policy of the Nixon administration, in which the United States no longer regarded its fundamental strategy as the containment of communism, but as a cooperative world order, in which Nixon and his chief adviser Henry Kissinger were focused on the broader constellation of forces and the bigger world powers. Nixon had ordered Kissinger to negotiate diplomatic policies with the Soviets, and later Vietnamese officials in Paris. Kissinger had already met, on several occasions, with North Vietnamese officials in Paris.

If nothing else, they all agreed that in the future the meeting tables would not be square, but round. By early May of 1969, the Paris Peace Talks officially began. Nixon also opened high-level contact with China. U.S. relations with the Soviet Union and China were of higher priority than South Vietnam in his mind. As it turned out, Kissinger ended up giving away the farm to North Vietnam. During the Peace Talks, he conceded that America should withdraw a substantial number of combat troops. (In so doing, this would eventually grease the wheels for an easy conquest of South Vietnam by the communist North.)

CHAPTER XX: SHORT-TIMER

An alcoholic uncle cautioned me, when I was a teenager, not to become a *reformed drunk* when I grew up and possibly become a regular drinker. A reformed drunk has truly little to say in conversation except to crow that he has been sober.

A reformed alcoholic remembers exactly the number of days and hours since, and will look at his wristwatch and continue, for instance, "... and fifteen minutes." Us guys in 'Nam must have sounded the same, gloating about being shot, regarding time remaining in-country, for example, "I've got fifty-six day and a wake-up."

The reformed drunk reciting days hours and minutes of sobriety, to the drinker sounds like an ostentatious blowhard. Similar for the guy who has three-hundred days or so remaining in-country, the short-timer in 'Nam, displaying a small space between thumb and finger, and ostentatiously carrying on about his good fortune, in comparison to your bad fortune, can be annoying.

In retrospect, I had made an unwise decision one day. After eleven months in-country, I received orders that when I returned to the States, I would be promoted to buck sergeant, and assigned as drill-sergeant for my remaining five-months in service. Within days of having received the orders, a young lieutenant from headquarters briefly visited me at the mortar emplacement. He told me that he was aware that I had just become a sergeant. He said had been assigned to recruit sergeants and officers in the division, encouraging them to extend their tour in Vietnam by seventy days, in remedy of a manpower shortage in leadership. I could remain in Dong Tam. The trade-off he told me that after those seventy days, I would be relieved from the service, and not have to go to Ft Benning as a drill sergeant. I did not have to think twice and readily signed up. I announced to the guys at the mortar emplacement my decision. Most of them thought I was nuts. I was a super-duper short timer for Christ Sake. With the recent explosion of the ammo dump, and notable increase in rocket attacks, Dong Tam was no longer a desirable assignment. But I had already signed up. It was early April 1969. I only wondered if I qualified for another R&R. Technically, my tour ended in June, and I had now volunteered for another tour of seventy days. It didn't hurt to ask.

One day I visited the division office that authorized R&Rs and asked for a week in Australia. The clerk I spoke to only glanced at the single page of my orders that I had signed up to extend my tour in 'Nam. He typed up the authorization. No question surfaced that I had used up my R&R allotment when I had gone to Hong Kong two months past. Record keeping was sloppy, and I felt I got away with murder.

CHAPTER XXI: R&R IN AUSTRALIA

The American airliner set down in Sydney with me aboard. The partly constructed Sydney opera house came into view, along with the hanger bridge that crossed Sydney Bay. Once we set down on the tarmac, I unbuckled my seatbelt, looking out the window at a welcome panorama of civilization in form of commercial and residential buildings, as opposed to warzone metal airport hangers and structures. I had arrived at heaven on earth. In a short time, I found myself transported by a hotel shuttle to a hotel at King's Cross venue, the heart of Sydney. The hotel, among several others, was recommended to us Americans as we disembarked. We would get a generous discount at those hotels. While checking in for a week, I was informed by the guy at the front desk that there were dances arranged for us Americans at a dancehall downtown every Friday.

When Friday rolled around in several days, I went to the dancehall by cab. I had no doubt that there were so many of us American soldiers arriving from 'Nam for R&R, we were being herded. But that didn't concern me. I was intent on having a good time –and I did. I met an attractive young girl named Cathy and brought her back to my hotel room. There she gave me a hit of LSD (Purple Haze). I didn't come on after a half an hour or so, and asked for another tab. She gave it to me. Within another half an hour, bricks began falling from the sky. I became extremely paranoid. I fled from the hotel room to the street and flagged down a cab, telling the driver to rush me to the nearest hospital. At emergency, I cried out that I had overdosed on LSD. The doctor informed me that there was no cure for LSD. While I was wringing my hands and convulsing, he called the police. They came to the hospital and took my name. As they were leaving, I ran out the door behind them. "Where are you going with my name. Give me my name back!" I insisted.

They decided I needed to be jailed and took me to the nearest one. Since I was an American, they called the FBI in downtown Sydney. Several FBI agents picked me up and took me to their office. They admonished me, saying that I represented poor diplomatic relations between the United States and Australia. They put me on an airliner back to 'Nam, several days short of my one-week R&R. I returned to my unit, the mortar emplacement, Headquarters platoon, 3rd/60th, Ninth Infantry Division.

CHAPTER XXII: VIETNAMIZATION

Settled back into the mortar barge groove, I divulged nothing to my platoon leader as to my R&R gone sour in Sydney. I felt embarrassed. Alex Kaufbush dropped in on me at the mortar barge.

Alex was our machine gunner in the Fourth Platoon, my previous post. He was the guy who manned our M-60 firepower, with an assistant who fed the belt of bullets. Alex was berthed for several weeks, at our company barracks in Dong Tam as outpatient with the field hospital. He told me that he had tossed a grenade during a firefight. The grenade bounced off the trunk of a coconut tree. He saw it land on the ground very much alive, and he ran for cover. The grenade exploded and subsequently peppered his ass with shrapnel. After telling me about that, he told me that Frank Fabian had been sent back to the States.

Meanwhile, us guys at the mortar emplacement had a transistor radio and listened to Armed Forces Radio Viet Nam every evening. Along with rock and roll, and jazz out of AFVN Radio in Saigon, the station broadcast news for US military in Vietnam, ranging from the Delta to the DMZ. The top of the news in early 1969 was de-Americanization, later coined Vietnamization. Early on, the news reported that a withdrawal of troops would begin in a month or so. In a brief time, the reports were that as a symbolic gesture, the planners at MACV in Saigon would soon decide on a contingency of one-hundred soldiers to take the lead going home early. These would be combat troops, not admin personnel. To get the most favorable attention of worldwide media, the troops would be regaled with new uniforms, spiff-up on American military pomp and pageantry for several weeks of training, and finally be flown to McChord Air Force Base, to a red-carpet welcome with a reception by a brass band. After several more days, AFRN announced that the one-hundred men would be chosen from the ranks of the Ninth Infantry Division. Us mortar men with Headquarters Company, $3^{rd}/60^{th}$, Ninth Infantry Division were excited to hear this news, but could not imagine what was in store. In less than a month, the one hundred (symbolic) troops would return home to much pomp and pageantry. Those troops chosen would include all of us in the mortar emplacement. During the weeklong celebration media stampeded to Dong Tam, the mortar emplacement became decommissioned. Our small platoon was put up in nearby area of barracks among the other troops that made up the one hundred *chosen ones*. The group began practicing army drills for our arrival at McCord Air Force Base. During these several weeks, while taking part in the drills, a lieutenant approached me. I recognized him as the same guy who had signed me up for an extension of my tour. He told me that I was being assigned to a detail at the battalion Headquarters. I let him know that I had been selected among the hundred to go home under the Vietnamization program. He shook his head and reminded me that I had extended my tour, that I was a month and a half indebted. The deal was without exception.

CHAPTER XXIII: ROCKET CITY

As a sergeant, I was given my own room at the end of a barracks that served as way lay accommodations for FNGs directly from the States. I was in a weeklong holding pattern for assignment. Meanwhile, Dong Tam came under increasing siege. Rocket attacks became a nightly event, longer in duration and more accurate in finding targets. Word had it that the Vietnamese barbers, PX workers and even janitors were working under pretense. They were VC spies, and the enemy was gaining critical knowledge of base camp infrastructure. They were bringing precisely mapped longitude/latitude coordinates back to their brothers-in-arms for the nightly rocket attacks.

The Forest of Darkness stronghold, it seemed, was overflowing throughout the Delta and most notably into places like American base camps. In the past, we had been going to them to pick a fight -a bungle in the jungle. The Forest of Darkness was now coming to us.

As a newly crowned buck sergeant, and no longer with a home on the mortar barge, division headquarters had a special job for me. My new commanding officer detailed me to mop-up duties. Myself and a half dozen or so assigned under me would go around the base camp, to places where someone had been reported killed in rocket strikes the night before and take the body to the hospital morgue (I finally got my chaplain's assistant job). At least I had finally become a short-timer, and let everyone I met know the days and hours. The detail included collecting personal effects and annotating them by pen on tags in connection with the body, to get the wallet, glasses, watch, camera etc. delivered to the next-of-kin along with the corpse.

CHAPTER XXIV: THE SILVER BIRD

In early August I was out-processed. At Ton Se Nhut airbase, they told me I should change into civies. We were warned that upon arriving at the stateside airports we would be yelled at and protestors would throw empty bottles from roadside debris as an insult to us guys who departed the airport in proud uniform.

The crowds were misinformed, not conscious that it was not us kids who were responsible for the war.

The Silver Bird lifted off from Tan Son Nhut that sunny August morning, yours truly homebound.

A FINAL NOTE

IN THE SUMMER OF 2021, my friend and fellow writer Alan Hodgkinson sent me the rough draft of THE FOREST OF DARKNESS. This was not unusual, since we had been reading and editing each other's work for years. Once I finished reading the manuscript, I sent it back to him with a number of suggestions, along with some of my own work. As the months passed and I did not hear back from him, I became alarmed. Despite my calls, I was not able to reach him. It was not until a year later that I learned of his untimely death. Since I still had the manuscript he had sent me, I felt that the best way to honor Alan's memory would be to publish it posthumously. I hope that wherever he is, my efforts will please him.

Carlos Rubio

About the Author

In the middle of actively protesting the Vietnam War in the late Sixties in San Francisco and Berkeley, Alan Hodgkinson was drafted. The Army sent him to the Mekong Delta where he served as a rifleman with the 9th Infantry Division. A graduate of California State University, he worked as a photojournalist for several years, then enrolled in Colorado State University's Graduate Writing Program. Afterwards, he joined the Peace Corps and was sent to Fiji, where he taught writing and literature at the University of the South Pacific. Alan lived in New Mexico until his death, where he spent his time writing. He published many short stories and newspaper articles about the war since returning in 1969. AFTER INCOMING, his first novel, was published in 2001. He was also the author of GATHERING MUSHROOM CLOUDS IN FORECAST (a memoir) and A SNIPER'S SUN. THE FOREST OF DARKNESS was his last book.